MW01115664

CONTENTS

ZETTELKASTEN MASTERY

Unlocking Creativity & Productivity and Taming Information Overload with Smart Notes

Raissa Gomez

No part of this book may be reproduced or transmitted in any form whatsoever, electronic, or mechanical, including photocopying, recording, or by any informational storage or retrieval system without express permission from the author.

Copyright © 2024 JNR Publishing

All rights reserved

INTRODUCTION: THE POWER OF SMART NOTE-TAKING IN THE MODERN AGE

In today's fast-paced, information-saturated world, the ability to effectively capture, organize, and leverage knowledge has become a crucial skill for personal and professional success. From students and researchers to entrepreneurs and business leaders, those who can harness the power of their ideas and insights are best positioned to thrive in an increasingly complex and competitive landscape.

Yet, despite the proliferation of productivity tools and technologies, many people struggle to keep up with the sheer volume of information they encounter daily. Traditional note-taking methods, such as jotting down bullet points or highlighting passages, often fail to provide the depth, clarity, and connectivity needed to transform raw information into actionable knowledge.

This is where the Zettelkasten method comes in. Developed by German sociologist Niklas Luhmann, this revolutionary approach to note-taking has helped countless individuals and organizations unlock their full potential for learning, creativity, and achievement. By creating a dynamic, interconnected web of ideas and insights, the Zettelkasten method enables users to not only store and retrieve information more effectively but also to generate new knowledge and breakthrough solutions.

In this book, we will explore the power and potential of smart note-taking through the lens of the Zettelkasten method. Drawing on the latest research in cognitive psychology, neuroscience, and information theory, we will delve into the principles and practices that make this approach so effective for learning, retention, and creative output.

But this book is more than just a theoretical exploration. It is also a practical guide, filled with concrete strategies, techniques, and tools for implementing the Zettelkasten method in your own life and work. Whether you're a student seeking to ace your exams, a researcher aiming to publish groundbreaking papers, or an entrepreneur striving to build a successful business, the insights and advice in these pages will help you harness the full power of your knowledge and ideas.

Throughout the book, we will place a special emphasis on the application of smart note-taking to the world of entrepreneurship and business. In today's knowledge-driven economy, the ability to effectively manage and leverage information is not just a nice-to-have skill but a critical competitive advantage. By adopting the Zettelkasten method, entrepreneurs and businesses can boost their productivity, creativity, and decision-making, while also fostering a culture of lifelong learning and innovation.

We will explore how entrepreneurs can use their Zettelkasten to capture and develop business ideas, conduct market research, and identify new opportunities. We'll discuss how teams and organizations can implement collaborative knowledge management systems based on the Zettelkasten principles, improving communication, coordination, and collective intelligence. And we'll learn from real-world case studies of entrepreneurs, writers, and creators who have used smart note-taking to achieve remarkable results.

Whether you're new to the concept of smart note-taking or a seasoned practitioner looking to take your skills to the next level, this book will provide you with the knowledge, tools, and inspiration you need to transform your relationship with information and unlock your full potential for learning, growth, and success.

So, let's dive in and discover the power of the Zettelkasten method for ourselves. With dedication, practice, and an open mind, you too can become a master of smart note-taking and a pioneer of knowledge-driven innovation. The journey towards a lifetime of learning and growth starts here, with the simple yet profound act of taking smart notes.

Part I: Understanding the Zettelkasten Method

CHAPTER 1: THE ORIGINS AND PHILOSOPHY OF THE ZETTELKASTEN METHOD

1.1 Niklas Luhmann: The Godfather of Smart Note-Taking

To truly understand the power and potential of the Zettelkasten method, we must first explore its origins in the life and work of Niklas Luhmann. Born in 1927 in Lüneburg, Germany, Luhmann was a prolific sociologist, philosopher, and intellectual who made significant contributions to systems theory, communication theory, and the study of social complexity.

But what set Luhmann apart from his peers was not just the depth and breadth of his intellectual output but the unusual method he used to produce it. Over the course of his career, Luhmann wrote more than 70 books and over 400 scholarly articles, many of which were groundbreaking in their respective fields. And he attributed much of this productivity to his unique approach to note-taking, which he called the Zettelkasten method.

At the heart of Luhmann's Zettelkasten was a vast collection of index cards, or "Zettel," which he used to capture and organize his thoughts, ideas, and insights. Each card contained a single piece of information, such as a quotation, a summary of an article, or a personal reflection. And crucially, each card was given a unique identifier and linked to other relevant cards in the collection, creating a complex web of associations and connections.

For Luhmann, the Zettelkasten was not just a tool for storing and retrieving information but a powerful catalyst for generating new knowledge and insights. By constantly adding to and recombining the cards in his collection, Luhmann was able to explore new ideas, uncover hidden patterns, and develop original theories that might never have emerged through linear, hierarchical thinking alone.

In many ways, Luhmann's Zettelkasten can be seen as an early precursor to the hyperlinked, networked structure of the internet and the World Wide Web. Just as web pages are connected to each other via hyperlinks, allowing users to navigate freely and discover new content, Luhmann's index cards were linked together in a non-linear, associative fashion, enabling him to follow his curiosity and explore new intellectual frontiers.

But the power of Luhmann's Zettelkasten went beyond just its technical structure. It was also a reflection of his deeper philosophical beliefs about the nature of knowledge, creativity, and the role of the individual in society. For Luhmann, the Zettelkasten was not just a personal tool but a model for how knowledge could be created, shared, and advanced in a complex, rapidly changing world.

1.2 The Principles of Atomicity, Connectivity, and Serendipity

At the core of the Zettelkasten method are three key principles that distinguish it from traditional note-taking approaches: atomicity, connectivity, and serendipity. By understanding and applying these principles in our own knowledge management practices, we can unlock the full potential of smart note-taking for learning, creativity, and innovation.

The first principle, atomicity, refers to the idea that each note in a Zettelkasten should contain a single, self-contained unit of information. Rather than capturing long, complex ideas or arguments, the Zettelkasten method encourages us to break down our thoughts into their most essential components, expressed in clear, concise language.

This atomicity serves several important functions. First, it makes our notes more modular and flexible, allowing us to easily combine and recombine them in new ways as our knowledge and understanding evolve. Second, it forces us to clarify our thinking and distill our ideas down to their core elements, which can help us identify gaps, inconsistencies, or areas for further exploration. And third, it makes our notes more accessible and reusable over time, as we can quickly scan and retrieve specific pieces of information without having to wade through long, unstructured passages of text.

The second principle, connectivity, emphasizes the importance of creating rich, meaningful connections between the individual notes in our Zettelkasten. Rather than organizing our notes in a rigid, hierarchical structure based on predefined categories or topics, the Zettelkasten method encourages us to link our notes together based on their inherent relationships and associations.

This connectivity can take many forms, from direct links between closely related ideas to more subtle, associative connections that span different domains or disciplines. By actively seeking out and creating these connections, we can begin to see our knowledge not as a static collection of facts and figures but as a dynamic, evolving network of interrelated concepts and insights.

The power of connectivity lies in its ability to help us uncover new patterns, relationships, and possibilities that might otherwise remain hidden. Just as the human brain relies on the complex web of connections between neurons to enable learning, memory, and creativity, a well-connected Zettelkasten can serve as a powerful catalyst for generating new ideas and insights.

The third principle, serendipity, highlights the importance of embracing unexpected discoveries and insights that emerge through the process of note-taking and knowledge management. Unlike traditional, goal-oriented approaches to learning and research, the Zettelkasten method encourages us to follow our curiosity and explore tangential ideas and connections, even if their immediate relevance or value is unclear.

This serendipitous approach can lead to surprising and valuable breakthroughs, as we stumble upon new ideas, perspectives, or solutions that we might never have encountered through more linear, focused thinking. By creating a system that is open to chance encounters and unplanned detours, we can cultivate a more flexible, adaptable mindset that is better suited to the complex, rapidly changing nature of modern knowledge work.

Together, these three principles form the foundation of the Zettelkasten method and distinguish it from more conventional approaches to note-taking and knowledge management. By embracing atomicity, connectivity, and serendipity in our own practices, we can begin to unlock the full potential of our minds and tap into a deeper, more generative mode of thinking and learning.

But to truly understand the power of the Zettelkasten method, we must also explore the psychological and scientific principles that underlie its effectiveness. In the next chapter, we will delve into the cognitive and neurological mechanisms that make smart note-taking such a powerful tool for learning, retention, and creative problem-solving.

CHAPTER 2: THE PSYCHOLOGY AND SCIENCE BEHIND EFFECTIVE NOTE-TAKING

2.1 Cognitive Benefits of Elaborative Encoding and Active Recall

At its core, the effectiveness of the Zettelkasten method lies in its ability to promote deeper, more meaningful learning and retention of information. By encouraging users to actively engage with their notes through techniques such as elaborative encoding and active recall, the Zettelkasten method helps to overcome the limitations of passive, rote memorization and enables a more robust, flexible understanding of complex ideas and concepts.

Elaborative encoding refers to the process of actively making connections between new information and existing knowledge, thereby creating a richer, more contextual memory trace. When we encounter a new idea or concept, our brains naturally try to make sense of it by relating it to what we already know. By explicitly articulating these connections in our notes, we can strengthen the associative links in our memory and make the new information more meaningful and memorable.

For example, let's say you come across a new business concept in your reading, such as the "lean startup" methodology. Rather than simply jotting down the definition and moving on, you might create a note that connects this idea to your existing knowledge of entrepreneurship, product development, and customer feedback. You might draw comparisons to other methodologies you're familiar with, highlight key differences or similarities, and reflect on how this new concept could apply to your own business ventures.

By engaging in this kind of elaborative encoding, you are not only deepening your understanding of the lean startup methodology itself but also integrating it into your broader knowledge base. This makes it more likely that you'll be able to recall and apply this concept in relevant situations, as it is now connected to a wider network of associations and experiences.

Active recall, on the other hand, refers to the process of actively retrieving information from memory, rather than simply re-reading or reviewing it passively. Research has shown that the act of recalling information from memory strengthens the neural connections associated with that information, making it more durable and accessible over time.

The Zettelkasten method promotes active recall in several ways. First, by breaking down complex ideas into atomic, self-contained notes, it encourages users to practice summarizing and synthesizing information in their own words. This act of translation and condensation requires a deeper engagement with the material than simply highlighting or copying verbatim, and it helps to cement the key ideas in memory.

Second, the process of creating and linking notes in a Zettelkasten requires users to actively search for and retrieve relevant information from their existing knowledge base. When deciding how to connect a new note to existing ones, users must mentally scan their prior knowledge, looking for patterns, similarities, and relationships. This process of active retrieval not only strengthens the connections between notes but also enhances the overall organization and accessibility of information in memory.

Third, the non-linear, networked structure of a Zettelkasten encourages users to revisit and engage with their notes in novel, unexpected ways. Rather than simply reviewing notes in the order they were created, users can follow associative links and explore tangential ideas, constantly refreshing and strengthening their memory of the key concepts and insights contained within.

Together, elaborative encoding and active recall form a powerful combination for deep, durable learning and retention. By intentionally connecting new information to prior knowledge and actively retrieving that information through the process of note-taking and linking, users of the Zettelkasten method can overcome the limitations of traditional, passive learning approaches and develop a more robust, flexible understanding of complex ideas and concepts.

2.2 The Role of Chunking, Spacing, and Interleaving in Learning and Retention

In addition to elaborative encoding and active recall, the Zettelkasten method also leverages several other key principles from cognitive psychology to enhance learning and retention. These include chunking, spacing, and interleaving, each of which plays a crucial role in how our brains process, store, and retrieve information over time.

Chunking refers to the process of breaking down complex information into smaller, more manageable units or "chunks." Our brains have a limited capacity for processing new information at once, and chunking allows us to efficiently organize and store related pieces of information together in memory.

The Zettelkasten method promotes chunking through its emphasis on atomic, self-contained notes. By breaking down complex ideas and arguments into smaller, more focused units, users can more easily process and retain the key insights and concepts. This is particularly important when dealing with dense, technical, or unfamiliar material, as it allows users to gradually build up their understanding piece by piece, rather than trying to grasp the entire complex idea at once.

Spacing, also known as distributed practice, refers to the idea that learning is more effective when it is spread out over time, rather than crammed into a single, intensive session. Research has consistently shown that spacing out learning sessions leads to better long-term retention and recall, as it allows time for the brain to consolidate and strengthen the neural connections associated with the learned material.

The Zettelkasten method encourages spacing through its emphasis on continuous, incremental note-taking and review. Rather than trying to capture and internalize all the relevant information on a topic in a single sitting, users are encouraged to engage with their notes regularly over time, gradually building up their knowledge and understanding through repeated exposure and elaboration.

Interleaving, a related concept, refers to the practice of mixing up different topics or skills during learning, rather than focusing on a single topic or skill at a time. By constantly switching between different ideas and contexts, learners are forced to actively distinguish between related concepts and practice applying their knowledge in novel situations.

The networked, associative structure of a Zettelkasten supports interleaving by encouraging users to explore connections and relationships between seemingly disparate ideas. As users navigate their web of notes, they are constantly exposed to a variety of topics and perspectives, which helps to strengthen their ability to transfer and apply their knowledge across different domains.

Example: Imagine you're an entrepreneur researching different marketing strategies for your new product. As you read various articles and case studies, you create atomic notes in your Zettelkasten on topics like social media advertising, content marketing, influencer partnerships, and email campaigns. By chunking this information into focused, self-contained notes, you can more easily process and retain the key insights from each approach.

As you continue to add notes on marketing over time, you are engaging in spaced learning, gradually building up your knowledge and expertise through repeated exposure and elaboration. And by linking your marketing notes to related concepts like customer psychology, branding, and analytics, you are interleaving your learning, developing a more flexible and transferable understanding of how marketing fits into the bigger picture of running a successful business.

2.3 The Importance of Metacognition and Self-Regulation in Knowledge Management

Beyond the cognitive principles discussed above, effective knowledge management also requires a strong sense of metacognition and self-regulation. Metacognition refers to the ability to think about and reflect on one's own thinking and learning processes, while self-regulation involves the ability to monitor, control, and adapt one's behavior and strategies in pursuit of learning goals.

The Zettelkasten method promotes metacognition by encouraging users to actively engage with their own learning and thinking processes. As users create and connect notes in their Zettelkasten, they are forced to reflect on their understanding of the material, identify gaps or areas of confusion, and make deliberate choices about how to organize and relate different pieces of information.

Example: As you're building your Zettelkasten on marketing strategies, you might notice that you have a lot of notes on social media advertising but comparatively few on email marketing. This realization might prompt you to seek out additional resources on email marketing to fill in the gaps in your knowledge, or to reflect on why you have prioritized social media in your learning so far.

Similarly, the Zettelkasten method supports self-regulation by providing users with a clear, external record of their learning progress and knowledge development over time. By regularly reviewing and engaging with their notes, users can track their own understanding, identify areas where they need to focus their efforts, and adapt their learning strategies accordingly.

Example: As you review your marketing notes, you might realize that you have a solid grasp of the basic principles and tactics but struggle to apply them to your specific business context. This insight might prompt you to seek out more practical, hands-on learning experiences, such as conducting market research or running small-scale experiments, to help bridge the gap between theory and practice.

Cultivating strong metacognitive and self-regulatory skills is essential for effective knowledge management in today's fast-paced, information-rich world. By providing a structured framework for reflection, self-assessment, and strategic learning, the Zettelkasten method empowers users to take control of their own knowledge development and adapt to the ever-changing demands of their personal and professional lives.

CHAPTER 3: ADVANTAGES OF THE ZETTELKASTEN METHOD OVER TRADITIONAL NOTE-TAKING

3.1 Overcoming the Limitations of Linear Thinking and Rigid Categorization

Traditional note-taking methods, such as outlining or summarizing, often rely on linear, hierarchical structures that can limit creativity and insight. By forcing ideas into predefined categories or sequences, these methods can make it difficult to see connections across different domains, explore alternative perspectives, or generate novel combinations of ideas.

The Zettelkasten method, in contrast, embraces a more fluid, non-linear approach to knowledge organization. Rather than trying to fit ideas into a rigid hierarchy or outline, the Zettelkasten encourages users to create a network of interconnected, atomic notes that can be freely associated and recombined in novel ways.

This non-linear structure allows for a more organic, emergent form of knowledge creation, where new ideas and insights can arise from the serendipitous collision of different concepts and perspectives. By breaking free from the constraints of traditional categorization, users can explore a wider range of connections and possibilities, leading to more creative and original thinking.

Example: Imagine you're an entrepreneur exploring new product ideas in the health and wellness space. With a traditional outlining approach, you might start by creating a hierarchical list of potential product categories, such as "fitness equipment," "nutrition supplements," and "mindfulness apps." While this structure can help you organize your thoughts, it may also limit your ability to see potential connections or opportunities that cut across these categories.

With a Zettelkasten approach, you might instead create a web of interconnected notes on various aspects of health and wellness, such as "exercise motivation," "gut-brain connection," "habit formation," and "stress reduction." As you explore the relationships between these different concepts, you may start to see new possibilities emerge, such as a product that combines physical activity with mindfulness practice, or a nutrition program that emphasizes the link between diet and mental health.

By embracing a more fluid, associative form of knowledge organization, the Zettelkasten method can help users break free from the limitations of linear thinking and rigid categorization, opening up new avenues for creative insight and innovation.

3.2 Facilitating Cross-Disciplinary Connections and Innovative Insights

In today's complex, interconnected world, many of the most important challenges and opportunities lie at the intersection of different fields and disciplines. Whether it's developing new technologies, solving social problems, or creating innovative business models, the ability to draw connections across diverse domains of knowledge is increasingly essential for success.

Traditional note-taking methods, which often emphasize a narrow, discipline-specific focus, can make it difficult to see these cross-disciplinary connections and insights. By siloing information into separate categories or folders, these methods can create artificial barriers between different areas of knowledge, limiting the potential for creative synthesis and breakthrough thinking.

The Zettelkasten method, on the other hand, actively encourages users to seek out and explore connections across different disciplines and domains. By creating a single, interconnected web of notes that spans a wide range of topics and ideas, users can more easily discover unexpected relationships and parallels between seemingly unrelated concepts.

This cross-disciplinary approach can lead to more innovative and original insights, as users are able to draw upon a diverse range of knowledge and perspectives to tackle complex problems and challenges. By breaking down the silos between different fields and disciplines, the Zettelkasten method can help users develop a more holistic, integrative understanding of the world, leading to more creative and effective solutions.

Example: Imagine you're a healthcare entrepreneur looking to develop new solutions for chronic disease management. With a traditional, discipline-specific approach to note-taking, you might focus narrowly on medical research and clinical best practices, missing out on potential insights from other relevant fields such as behavioral psychology, data analytics, or user experience design.

With a Zettelkasten approach, you might create a web of notes that spans all of these different domains, exploring connections and synergies between them. As you link your notes on chronic disease management to related concepts like habit formation, personalized medicine, and patient engagement, you may start to see new possibilities emerge, such as a mobile app that uses gamification and social support to help patients stick to their treatment plans, or a data-driven platform that helps doctors tailor interventions to individual patient needs and preferences.

By facilitating cross-disciplinary connections and insights, the

Zettelkasten method can help users break out of narrow, siloed ways of thinking and develop more creative, innovative solutions to complex problems.

3.3 Enabling Incremental and Iterative Progress Towards Long-Term Goals

Another key advantage of the Zettelkasten method is its ability to support incremental, iterative progress towards long-term learning and creative goals. Unlike traditional note-taking approaches, which often emphasize discrete, one-time acts of capturing and storing information, the Zettelkasten method is designed to be a living, evolving system that grows and adapts over time.

By encouraging users to continually add to, refine, and connect their notes, the Zettelkasten method enables a more gradual, iterative approach to knowledge creation and skill development. Rather than trying to learn everything at once or tackle complex projects in a single, linear sequence, users can make steady, incremental progress by building up their knowledge base one note at a time.

This incremental approach can be particularly valuable for entrepreneurs and professionals tackling long-term, open-ended challenges such as building a business, developing a new product line, or mastering a complex skill set. By breaking these larger goals down into smaller, more manageable pieces and capturing insights and ideas along the way, users can maintain momentum and motivation even in the face of setbacks or uncertainty.

Example: Imagine you're an entrepreneur working to build a successful e-commerce business from scratch. With a traditional, project-based approach to learning and planning, you might try to map out every step of the process in advance, from product development to marketing to sales, and then work through each step in a linear, sequential fashion.

With a Zettelkasten approach, you might instead focus on building up your knowledge and expertise incrementally over time, capturing insights and ideas as you go. As you read books and articles on e-commerce strategies, attend workshops and conferences, and experiment with different tactics and approaches, you can create a growing web of notes that reflect your evolving understanding of the field.

Over time, as your Zettelkasten grows and develops, you can start to see patterns and connections emerge that can inform your business strategy and decision-making. By linking your notes on customer needs and preferences to your notes on product design and development, for example, you might identify new opportunities to create value and differentiate your brand. Or by connecting your notes on marketing channels and tactics to your notes on analytics and metrics, you might discover new ways to optimize your campaigns and improve your ROI.

By enabling this kind of incremental, iterative progress towards long-term goals, the Zettelkasten method can help entrepreneurs and professionals stay agile and adaptable in the face of changing circumstances and new challenges. Rather than trying to predict and control every aspect of the journey in advance, users can focus on learning and growing each day, trusting that their knowledge and skills will compound over time to help them achieve their larger aims and ambitions.

Part II: Implementing the Zettelkasten Method in Practice

CHAPTER 4: GETTING STARTED WITH YOUR ZETTELKASTEN - TOOLS AND SETUP

4.1 Choosing the Right Medium - Analog vs. Digital Options

One of the first decisions you'll need to make when setting up your Zettelkasten is choosing the right medium for capturing and organizing your notes. While the original Zettelkasten system used by Niklas Luhmann was entirely analog, consisting of physical index cards and wooden boxes, today's users have a wide range of digital tools and platforms to choose from as well.

Each medium has its own advantages and trade-offs, and the right choice for you will depend on your personal preferences, working style, and specific needs and goals. Let's take a closer look at some of the key considerations for each option:

Analog Zettelkasten:

- *Advantages:* Many users find that the tactile, physical nature of handwriting notes on index cards helps them process and retain information more effectively than typing on a keyboard. Analog systems can also be less distracting and more conducive to deep, focused thinking, as they are not subject to the same digital notifications and interruptions as electronic devices.

- *Disadvantages:* Analog systems can be more cumbersome and time-consuming to maintain than digital ones, as they require physical storage space and manual organization and retrieval of notes. They can also be more difficult to search, filter, and link together than digital notes, which can limit their scalability and flexibility over time.

Digital Zettelkasten:

- *Advantages:* Digital tools offer a wide range of features and functionalities that can streamline and enhance the Zettelkasten process, from full-text search and tagging to automatic backlinks and graph visualization. They also make it easy to access and sync your notes across multiple devices, collaborate with others, and back up your data to prevent loss or damage.

- *Disadvantages:* Digital systems can be more prone to distraction and information overload than analog ones, as users may be tempted to constantly check for updates or notifications. They can also be more vulnerable to technical glitches, software updates, or platform obsolescence, which can disrupt or compromise the long-term stability and accessibility of your notes.

Ultimately, the best medium for your Zettelkasten will depend on your individual needs and preferences as a learner and creator. Some users may prefer the simplicity and focus of an analog system, while others may value the convenience and flexibility of digital tools. Still, others may opt for a hybrid approach, using both physical and digital notes in combination to get the best of both worlds.

Example: Imagine you're a freelance writer and researcher who frequently works on long-form projects such as books, whitepapers, and feature articles. You may find that an analog Zettelkasten, consisting of physical index cards and a filing cabinet, helps you stay focused and avoid digital distractions during the deep work of reading, thinking, and writing.

At the same time, you may also use a digital tool like Evernote or Roam Research to capture and organize shorter, more ephemeral notes, such as quotes, ideas, or references that you come across while browsing the web or reading on your phone. By syncing these digital notes with your analog system, you can create a seamless, integrated workflow that leverages the strengths of both mediums.

4.2 Essential Features and Characteristics of Effective Zettelkasten Software

If you do decide to use a digital tool for your Zettelkasten, there are several essential features and characteristics to look for to ensure a smooth, effective workflow. While the specific tools and platforms available are constantly evolving, here are some key considerations to keep in mind:

1. **Plaintext format:** Look for a tool that stores your notes in a simple, portable plaintext format such as Markdown or TXT, rather than a proprietary or encrypted format. This ensures that your notes will be accessible and future-proof, even if the specific software you're using becomes obsolete or unsupported over time.

2. **Atomic notes:** Choose a tool that supports the creation of small, self-contained notes, rather than long, monolithic documents. This allows for greater flexibility and modularity in linking and combining ideas, and makes it easier to create a networked structure of knowledge over time.

3. **Linking and backlinks:** A key feature of any effective Zettelkasten tool is the ability to easily create links between notes, and to see all the notes that link back to a given note (known as "backlinks"). This allows for a more organic, associative form of knowledge organization and discovery, and helps users explore connections and relationships across different areas of

their knowledge base.

4. **Search and filtering:** As your Zettelkasten grows over time, it becomes increasingly important to be able to quickly search and filter your notes to find relevant information. Look for a tool with robust search functionality, including full-text search, tag-based filtering, and the ability to save and reuse complex search queries.

5. **Customization and extensibility:** Every user's Zettelkasten workflow is unique, so it's important to choose a tool that allows for a high degree of customization and extensibility. This might include the ability to create custom templates, use plugins or add-ons, or integrate with other tools and platforms that you use for research, writing, or project management.

Example: Imagine you're a software developer looking to create a Zettelkasten for managing your knowledge and learning related to programming languages, frameworks, and best practices. You might choose a tool like Obsidian or Foam, which are designed specifically for plaintext, atomic note-taking and support features like linking, backlinks, and graph visualization.

As you capture notes on different topics, from JavaScript syntax to database design to agile development methodologies, you can use tags and links to create a networked structure of knowledge that reflects your evolving understanding of the field.

For example, you might create a note on "JavaScript Promises" that links to other notes on topics like "Asynchronous Programming," "Callbacks," and "Error Handling." As you come across new information or insights related to Promises, you can easily add them to your existing note or create new linked notes, building up a rich web of interconnected knowledge over time.

With the help of search and filtering features, you can quickly find and retrieve relevant notes as needed, whether you're working on a specific project, preparing for a job interview, or simply exploring new areas of interest. And by choosing a tool with good customization and extensibility options, you can adapt and evolve your Zettelkasten workflow as your needs and goals change over time, ensuring that it remains a valuable and relevant resource for your ongoing learning and growth.

4.3 Creating a Consistent and Scalable Structure for Your Notes

Once you've chosen your tools and platform, the next step in setting up your Zettelkasten is to create a consistent and scalable structure for your notes. This involves establishing clear conventions and guidelines for how you will capture, organize, and link your ideas over time, in order to create a coherent and navigable web of knowledge.

Here are some key elements to consider when creating a structure for your Zettelkasten:

1. **Unique identifiers:** Assign a unique identifier to each note, such as a timestamp or a sequential number, to make it easy to reference and link to specific notes across your system. This identifier should be independent of the note's title or content, so that it remains stable even if the note itself changes over time.

2. **Consistent formatting:** Establish a consistent format for your notes, including elements like headers, bullet points, and emphasis, to make them easy to read and scan. Use a simple, lightweight markup language like Markdown to ensure that your formatting is portable and future-proof.

3. **Linking conventions:** Develop clear conventions for how you will link notes together, such as using double square brackets ([[note-id]]) or a specific syntax for tags. Be consistent in your use of these conventions to ensure that your links remain valid and functional over time.

4. **Organizational principles:** Decide on the key organizational principles that will guide how you

structure and navigate your Zettelkasten. This might include things like using a hierarchical folder structure, maintaining a central index or table of contents, or relying on tags and links to create a more fluid, associative structure.

5. **Naming conventions:** Establish clear naming conventions for your notes and folders, to make them easy to find and identify at a glance. Use descriptive, concise titles that reflect the main idea or topic of each note, and avoid using generic or vague names that could apply to multiple notes.

Example: Let's say you're a marketer setting up a Zettelkasten to capture your knowledge and ideas related to content strategy, social media, and email marketing. You might establish a structure that looks something like this:

- Each note is stored as a plaintext file with a unique identifier, such as "202305010001" for the first note created on May 1, 2023.

- Notes are formatted using Markdown, with consistent use of headers, bullet points, and emphasis to create a clear visual hierarchy.

- Links between notes are created using double square brackets, such as [[202305010002]], and tags are added using a hash symbol, such as #content-strategy or #email-marketing.

- Notes are organized into a hierarchical folder structure, with top-level folders for each main area of focus (e.g. "Content Strategy," "Social Media," "Email Marketing") and sub-folders for more specific topics or projects as needed.

- Note titles are concise and descriptive, such as "The Role of Storytelling in Content Marketing" or "Best Practices for Email Subject Lines," and avoid generic or redundant phrases like "Notes on..." or "Thoughts about..."

By establishing a clear and consistent structure for your Zettelkasten from the outset, you can create a scalable and maintainable system that will support your learning and growth over time. As you add more notes and explore new areas of knowledge, having a well-defined structure in place will make it easier to integrate new ideas and insights into your existing web of knowledge, and to find and retrieve relevant information when you need it.

CHAPTER 5: THE ART OF CREATING EFFECTIVE ZETTEL NOTES

5.1 Capturing Fleeting Notes - Techniques for Recording Insights on the Go

The first step in creating a Zettelkasten is to capture the fleeting notes and ideas that come to you throughout the day, whether you're reading a book, attending a meeting, or simply going for a walk. These notes are often quick, rough, and incomplete, but they serve as the raw material for your more developed, polished notes later on.

Here are some techniques for effectively capturing fleeting notes on the go:

1. **Always be ready:** Keep a notebook, index card, or digital note-taking app with you at all times, so you can quickly jot down ideas as they come to you. Don't worry about formatting or organization at this stage - the key is to get the idea down before it slips away.

2. **Focus on key concepts and insights:** When capturing fleeting notes, try to focus on the core ideas and insights that stand out to you, rather than getting bogged down in details or trying to capture everything verbatim. Use shorthand, abbreviations, or sketches to quickly convey

the essence of the idea.

3. **Use prompts and questions:** If you're having trouble getting started, try using prompts or questions to stimulate your thinking and generate new ideas. For example, you might ask yourself "What surprised me about this?" or "How does this relate to my current project or goal?"

4. **Capture context and metadata:** In addition to the core idea or insight, try to capture any relevant context or metadata that will help you make sense of the note later on. This might include things like the source of the idea (e.g. a book title or conversation), the date and time, or any related thoughts or associations that come to mind.

5. **Review and process regularly:** Make a habit of regularly reviewing and processing your fleeting notes, ideally within a day or two of capturing them. This will help you identify the most promising ideas to develop further, and ensure that you don't lose track of any valuable insights over time.

Example: Let's say you're a product manager attending a conference on user experience design. During a particularly interesting talk, you jot down the following fleeting note on your phone:

"Ethnographic research - observe users in their natural environment, not just lab setting. Helps uncover hidden needs & pain points. Could be useful for our onboarding flow redesign project?"

This note captures the core idea (ethnographic research), the context (a conference talk), and a potential application or connection to your own work (the onboarding flow redesign project). By quickly capturing this insight in the moment, you can ensure that you don't forget it later on, and can come back to it when you have more time to process and develop the idea further.

5.2 Crafting Literature Notes - Strategies for

Processing and Summarizing Sources

Once you've captured your fleeting notes, the next step is to process and summarize the sources and ideas you've collected, turning them into more structured, polished literature notes. Literature notes are still relatively brief and concise, but they aim to capture the key ideas and arguments from a particular source in a more coherent and organized way.

Here are some strategies for crafting effective literature notes:

1. **Summarize in your own words:** When processing a source, try to summarize the main ideas and arguments in your own words, rather than simply copying and pasting quotes or excerpts. This will help you internalize and engage with the material more deeply, and make it easier to integrate the ideas into your own thinking later on.

2. **Focus on key takeaways and insights:** Rather than trying to capture every detail or nuance from a source, focus on the key takeaways and insights that are most relevant or interesting to you. Look for the main arguments, evidence, and conclusions that stand out, and the ideas that spark new connections or questions in your mind.

3. **Use a consistent structure:** To make your literature notes more organized and easier to review later on, try to use a consistent structure or template for each one. This might include elements like the source title and author, the main ideas or arguments, any key quotes or examples, and your own thoughts or reflections on the material.

4. **Link to related notes:** As you create your literature notes, look for opportunities to link them to other relevant notes in your Zettelkasten, using the linking conventions you established in your setup. This will help you start to build up a network of connections and

associations between different ideas and sources.

5. **Iterate and refine:** Don't worry about getting your literature notes perfect on the first try. As you continue to process and engage with the material, you may find that your understanding of the ideas evolves or changes over time. Feel free to go back and refine or update your notes as needed, to reflect your latest thinking and insights.

Example: Let's say you're reading a book on marketing psychology, and you come across a section on the concept of social proof. You might create a literature note that looks something like this:

Title: Social Proof: The Power of Consensus in Marketing Source: "Influence: The Psychology of Persuasion" by Robert Cialdini Main Ideas:

- Social proof is the idea that people are more likely to take a particular action if they see others doing it first.
- Examples include customer reviews, celebrity endorsements, and "wisdom of the crowd" effects.
- Social proof is particularly effective when people are uncertain or in unfamiliar situations.
- Marketers can leverage social proof by highlighting customer testimonials, showcasing social media followers/engagement, and using phrases like "best-selling" or "most popular."

Connections:

- Relates to idea of [[202305010023]] on the importance of trust and credibility in marketing.
- Could be useful for [[202305020015]] project on redesigning our product pages to increase conversions.

Reflection:

- Makes sense intuitively, but I wonder how social proof interacts with other factors like price, branding, etc.

Would be interesting to test different types of social proof in our own marketing and see what works best.

By summarizing the key ideas from the source, linking them to related notes, and reflecting on the implications and potential applications of the concept, this literature note captures the essence of the material in a concise and meaningful way, while also laying the groundwork for further exploration and development of the ideas.

5.3 Transforming Ideas into Permanent Notes - The Heart of the Zettelkasten Method

The final and most important step in the Zettelkasten process is to transform the fleeting notes and literature notes you've captured into permanent notes that represent your own thinking and original insights on a topic. Permanent notes are the heart of your Zettelkasten, the distilled essence of your learning and knowledge creation process.

Here are some key principles and techniques for creating effective permanent notes:

1. **Synthesize and integrate:** Permanent notes should not simply summarize or regurgitate the ideas from your fleeting and literature notes, but rather synthesize and integrate them into your own original thinking. Look for patterns, connections, and contradictions across different sources and ideas, and use them to develop your own unique perspective or argument.

2. **Express a single, atomic idea:** Each permanent note should express a single, self-contained idea or insight that can stand on its own, without depending on the context of other notes. Aim to make each note as clear, concise, and standalone as possible, so that it can be easily reused and recombined with other notes in different contexts.

3. **Use your own voice and perspective:** Permanent notes should be written in your own words and reflect your

own unique voice, style, and perspective on the topic. Don't be afraid to inject your personality, opinions, or experiences into your notes, as this will make them more engaging and memorable both for yourself and for others who might read them.

4. **Link liberally:** One of the key strengths of the Zettelkasten method is the ability to create rich, interconnected webs of ideas and knowledge. As you create your permanent notes, look for opportunities to link them to other related notes in your system, using the linking conventions you established in your setup. The more connections you create, the more powerful and generative your Zettelkasten will become over time.

5. **Iterate and evolve:** Just like your literature notes, your permanent notes should be seen as living, evolving entities that can change and grow over time as your understanding of a topic deepens. Don't be afraid to go back and refine, update, or even split or merge your permanent notes as needed, to reflect your latest thinking and insights.

Example: Building on the example of social proof from the previous section, let's say you've collected a few more fleeting and literature notes on the topic, and you're ready to synthesize them into a permanent note. It might look something like this:

Title: The Power of Social Proof in Marketing Tags: #marketing #psychology #influence

Social proof is a powerful psychological principle that can be leveraged to increase trust, credibility, and conversions in marketing. At its core, social proof is based on the idea that people are more likely to take a particular action if they see others doing it first, particularly in situations of uncertainty or unfamiliarity ([[202305030012]]).

There are many different types of social proof that marketers can use, from customer reviews and testimonials

([[202305030014]]) to celebrity endorsements and influencer marketing ([[202305030018]]). The key is to find the right type of social proof for your particular audience and context, and to use it in a way that feels authentic and relevant to their needs and interests.

One potential downside of social proof is that it can sometimes lead to herd mentality or groupthink, where people blindly follow the crowd without considering their own individual preferences or needs ([[202305030022]]). As marketers, we need to be aware of this risk and use social proof in a way that empowers and informs our audiences, rather than manipulating or misleading them.

Ultimately, the power of social proof lies in its ability to tap into our deep-seated human desire for connection, belonging, and validation from others. By leveraging this principle in a thoughtful and strategic way, we can build stronger, more authentic relationships with our customers and create marketing messages that truly resonate and inspire action.

Connections:

- [[202305010023]] Trust and credibility in marketing
- [[202305020015]] Redesigning product pages for conversions
- [[202305030016]] The role of emotions in consumer decision-making

In this permanent note, the ideas from the previous literature note are synthesized and integrated with additional insights and perspectives from other notes, creating a more comprehensive and nuanced understanding of the concept of social proof. The note expresses a clear, standalone idea, written in the author's own voice and perspective, and links liberally to other related notes to create a rich web of connections and associations.

By creating permanent notes like this on a regular basis, you can gradually build up a powerful, interconnected web of knowledge that reflects your unique interests, insights, and expertise. Over time, as you continue to add to and refine your Zettelkasten, you'll find that it becomes an invaluable resource for your ongoing learning, creativity, and personal and professional growth.

CHAPTER 6: DEVELOPING YOUR ZETTELKASTEN WORKFLOW - FROM CAPTURE TO CREATION

6.1 Establishing a Regular Review and Maintenance Schedule

One of the key principles of the Zettelkasten method is that it is a living, dynamic system that requires regular attention and maintenance to stay healthy and productive over time. Just like a garden needs consistent watering, pruning, and fertilizing to thrive, your Zettelkasten needs regular review and upkeep to remain a valuable and generative tool for your learning and creativity.

Here are some tips for establishing a regular review and maintenance schedule for your Zettelkasten:

1. **Set aside dedicated time:** Block out regular time in your schedule for reviewing and maintaining your Zettelkasten, whether it's daily, weekly, or monthly. Treat this time as a sacred commitment to your

own learning and growth, and protect it from other distractions or obligations.

2. **Review new notes:** Start each maintenance session by reviewing any new fleeting notes, literature notes, or permanent notes you've captured since your last review. Look for any new insights, connections, or questions that emerge, and consider how they fit into the broader context of your existing knowledge and interests.

3. **Prune and consolidate:** As you review your notes, look for any that are redundant, outdated, or no longer relevant to your current thinking or goals. Don't be afraid to delete or archive these notes to keep your system lean and focused. Similarly, look for opportunities to consolidate related notes or ideas into a single, more comprehensive note.

4. **Refine and update:** Look for opportunities to refine or update your existing notes based on new information, insights, or perspectives you've gained since creating them. This might involve adding new links, revising your arguments or examples, or splitting a note into multiple smaller notes to better capture the nuances of an idea.

5. **Explore and create:** Use your maintenance sessions as an opportunity to explore new connections and ideas within your Zettelkasten. Follow the links between notes, look for patterns or themes that emerge, and consider how you might combine or build upon existing ideas to create something new and original. Capture any new insights or ideas that arise as fleeting notes or permanent notes to continue growing your knowledge base.

Example: Let's say you're a writer and researcher who maintains a Zettelkasten on various topics related to your work. You might establish a weekly maintenance schedule that looks something like this:

- Every Monday morning, block out an hour to review any new notes you've captured in the past week. Tag and link these notes as appropriate, and consider how they fit into your existing knowledge structure.

- Every other Wednesday afternoon, spend 30 minutes pruning and consolidating your notes. Look for any notes that are no longer relevant or useful, and either delete them or combine them with other related notes to create a more streamlined and focused system.

- Every Friday afternoon, set aside an hour for deep exploration and creation within your Zettelkasten. Choose a specific topic or question to investigate, and follow the links and connections between your notes to see what new insights or ideas emerge. Capture any promising leads as new permanent notes, and consider how you might develop them further in future writing or research projects.

By establishing a regular maintenance schedule like this, you can ensure that your Zettelkasten remains a dynamic, generative tool for your ongoing learning and creativity. Over time, as you continue to refine and expand your knowledge base, you'll likely find that your maintenance sessions become more efficient and productive, as the structure and organization of your Zettelkasten becomes more intuitive and ingrained.

6.2 Techniques for Interlinking and Crosslinking Your Notes

One of the key strengths of the Zettelkasten method is its emphasis on creating rich, interconnected webs of knowledge through the use of links and associations between notes. By intentionally linking and crosslinking your notes, you can create a more powerful and generative system that surfaces new insights, connections, and creative possibilities over time.

Here are some techniques for interlinking and crosslinking your notes effectively:

1. **Link as you write:** As you create new permanent notes, look for opportunities to link them to existing notes in your Zettelkasten. This might involve linking to notes that explore similar themes or ideas, notes that provide supporting evidence or examples, or notes that offer contrasting or complementary perspectives.

2. **Use descriptive link text:** When creating a link, use descriptive, meaningful link text that clarifies the nature of the connection between the two notes. For example, instead of just linking to "[[202305030014]]", you might link to "[[202305030014|The role of customer reviews in building social proof]]". This makes it easier to understand the context and significance of the link at a glance.

3. **Create hub notes:** As you develop clusters of related notes around a particular topic or theme, consider creating "hub notes" that serve as central points of connection and navigation. These notes can provide an overview of the key ideas and subthemes within a particular area, and link out to more specific or detailed notes for further exploration.

4. **Use tags and indexes:** In addition to direct links between notes, consider using tags and indexes to create higher-level connections and associations. For example, you might tag all notes related to a particular project or area of interest with a common keyword, or create an index note that lists all the notes related to a particular theme or question.

5. **Explore multiple pathways:** When exploring your Zettelkasten, don't just follow the obvious or direct links between notes. Look for opportunities to create new, unexpected connections by following multiple pathways or tangents, and seeing where they lead. This

can often surface new insights or creative possibilities that you might not have discovered through a more linear or hierarchical approach.

Example: Let's say you're continuing to develop your Zettelkasten around the theme of marketing psychology and influence. As you create new notes on topics like scarcity, authority, and reciprocity, you might look for opportunities to link them to your existing notes on social proof:

- In your note on scarcity, you might link to your social proof note as an example of how scarcity can be used to create a sense of urgency or demand: "[[202305030012| Social proof can also be used to create a sense of scarcity, by highlighting how many other people are using or buying a particular product]]."
- In your note on authority, you might link to your social proof note as a way of establishing credibility and trust: "[[202305030012|Social proof from respected experts or authorities can be particularly powerful in establishing trust and credibility with an audience]]."
- In your note on reciprocity, you might link to your social proof note as an example of how social norms and obligations can influence behavior: "[[202305030012| Social proof can create a sense of social obligation or pressure to conform, similar to the principle of reciprocity]]."

As you continue to create these kinds of connections and associations between your notes, you might also consider creating a hub note on "Principles of Influence in Marketing" that provides an overview of the key concepts and links out to your individual notes on social proof, scarcity, authority, reciprocity, and other related ideas.

By intentionally interlinking and crosslinking your notes in this way, you can create a richer, more dynamic knowledge base that surfaces new insights and connections over time. As you explore the multiple pathways and associations between your ideas, you'll likely find that your understanding of the topic becomes deeper and more nuanced, and that new creative possibilities and applications emerge.

6.3 Using Outlining and Mapping Tools to Structure Your Ideas

While the core of the Zettelkasten method is the creation and linking of individual notes, there are also times when it can be helpful to step back and see the bigger picture of how your ideas fit together. This is where outlining and mapping tools can come in handy, allowing you to visualize and structure your notes in new and meaningful ways.

Here are some ways you can use outlining and mapping tools to support your Zettelkasten workflow:

1. **Create topic outlines:** As you develop clusters of notes around a particular topic or theme, consider using an outlining tool to create a high-level overview of the key ideas and sub-topics within that area. This can help you see the logical structure and progression of your thinking, and identify any gaps or areas that need further development.

2. **Map out arguments and narratives:** When working on a specific writing or research project, use an outlining tool to map out the main arguments, evidence, and examples you want to include. As you review your notes, look for the most relevant and compelling ideas to include in your outline, and consider how they can be structured and sequenced for maximum impact.

3. **Visualize connections and relationships:** In addition to traditional hierarchical outlines, consider using mind mapping or concept mapping tools to visualize the connections and relationships between your notes in a more free-form, associative way. This can be particularly helpful for exploring new creative possibilities or

identifying unexpected connections between seemingly disparate ideas.

4. **Integrate with your Zettelkasten:** Look for outlining and mapping tools that integrate seamlessly with your Zettelkasten, allowing you to easily link and reference individual notes within your outlines and maps. Some Zettelkasten-specific tools like Obsidian and Roam Research have built-in outlining and mapping features, while others can be integrated with external tools like Workflowy or MindMeister.

5. **Iterate and evolve:** Just like your Zettelkasten itself, your outlines and maps should be seen as living, evolving documents that can change and adapt over time as your thinking and understanding develops. Don't be afraid to revise, refine, or completely restructure your outlines and maps as needed to better capture your current knowledge and insights.

Example: Let's say you're using your marketing psychology Zettelkasten to develop a blog post on the top five principles of influence in marketing. You might start by creating a high-level outline of the key points you want to cover:

- Introduction
  - Hook: The power of influence in marketing
  - Thesis: Top 5 principles of influence every marketer should know
- Principle 1: Social Proof
  - Definition and examples
  - How to use social proof effectively
  - [[202305030012|The Power of Social Proof in Marketing]]
- Principle 2: Scarcity
  - Definition and examples
  - How to use scarcity effectively

- [[202305040033|The Psychology of Scarcity in Marketing]]
- Principle 3: Authority
  - Definition and examples
  - How to use authority effectively
  - [[202305050021|Establishing Authority and Credibility in Marketing]]
- Principle 4: Reciprocity
  - Definition and examples
  - How to use reciprocity effectively
  - [[202305060008|The Reciprocity Principle in Marketing and Sales]]
- Principle 5: Consistency and Commitment
  - Definition and examples
  - How to use consistency and commitment effectively
  - [[202305070002|Consistency and Commitment in Marketing Psychology]]
- Conclusion
  - Recap of key principles
  - Call-to-action: How to apply these principles in your own marketing efforts

As you develop this outline, you might link to specific notes within your Zettelkasten that provide more detail or supporting examples for each principle. You might also use a mind mapping tool to explore the connections and relationships between these principles, and identify any common themes or patterns that emerge.

For example, you might create a mind map that shows how social proof, authority, and consistency/commitment are all ways of leveraging social influence and norms, while scarcity and reciprocity tap into more individual psychological drives and needs. This might spark new insights or ideas for your blog post, such as discussing how these principles can be combined or layered for maximum impact.

By using outlining and mapping tools in conjunction with your Zettelkasten, you can create a more powerful and integrated system for developing and structuring your ideas. Whether you're working on a specific writing project, exploring a new area of interest, or simply trying to make sense of the connections and patterns within your knowledge base, these tools can help you see the bigger picture and identify new possibilities for growth and creation.

CHAPTER 7: LEVERAGING YOUR ZETTELKASTEN FOR WRITING AND CONTENT CREATION

7.1 Generating Ideas and Overcoming Writer's Block with Your Slip Box

One of the greatest challenges for any writer or content creator is coming up with fresh, compelling ideas on a regular basis. Whether you're working on a blog post, article, book, or other project, it's easy to feel stuck or uninspired, staring at a blank page with no clear direction or motivation.

This is where your Zettelkasten can be an invaluable tool for generating ideas and overcoming writer's block. By leveraging the rich web of notes, connections, and insights you've built up over time, you can quickly and easily find new angles, examples, and perspectives to inform and inspire your writing.

Here are some tips for using your Zettelkasten to generate ideas and overcome writer's block:

1. **Start with a question or theme:** When you're feeling stuck, start by identifying a specific question, theme, or topic you want to explore in your writing. This could be something broad and open-ended, like "What are the key

trends shaping the future of my industry?" or something more focused and specific, like "How can I use social proof to increase conversions on my product page?"

2. **Explore related notes:** Once you have a question or theme in mind, start exploring your Zettelkasten for notes and ideas that relate to that topic. Use the search function to find relevant keywords and phrases, follow links and tags to discover connected ideas, and browse your index or table of contents to identify promising areas for further exploration.

3. **Look for patterns and connections:** As you review your notes, look for patterns, themes, and connections that emerge across different ideas and sources. What common threads or arguments seem to run through multiple notes? What contrasts or contradictions do you notice between different perspectives or examples? How might these patterns and connections suggest new angles or approaches for your writing?

4. **Capture new ideas and insights:** As you explore your Zettelkasten, capture any new ideas, questions, or insights that arise in the form of fleeting notes or permanent notes. These could be potential angles or arguments for your writing, examples or case studies to illustrate your points, or simply new directions for further research and exploration.

5. **Outline and structure your ideas:** Once you have a collection of relevant notes and ideas, use an outlining or mapping tool to start structuring and organizing your thoughts into a coherent narrative or argument. Consider how different ideas and examples might fit together logically, what order or sequence would be most effective for presenting your points, and what key takeaways or conclusions you want your readers to come away with.

Example: Let's say you're a freelance writer working on an article about the benefits of a plant-based diet, but you're feeling stuck and uninspired. You might start by exploring your Zettelkasten for notes related to plant-based nutrition, looking for key themes, arguments, and examples that stand out.

As you review your notes, you might notice several recurring ideas and patterns:

- Multiple studies showing the health benefits of plant-based diets for reducing the risk of chronic diseases like heart disease, diabetes, and certain cancers ([[202301150023]], [[202302100018]], [[202303250007]])

- Personal anecdotes and case studies of individuals who have experienced significant health improvements after switching to a plant-based diet ([[202301300012]], [[202302200035]], [[202303050029]])

- Discussions of the environmental and ethical benefits of plant-based eating, such as reducing greenhouse gas emissions and animal suffering ([[202301200041]], [[202302050016]], [[202303150008]])

Seeing these patterns and connections, you might start to outline a potential structure for your article:

1. Introduction
    - Hook: Personal story of health transformation through plant-based eating
    - Thesis: Plant-based diets offer significant health, environmental, and ethical benefits

2. Health Benefits
    - Overview of key studies and research findings
    - Examples of specific health outcomes (e.g. lower risk of heart disease, diabetes, cancer)
    - Personal anecdotes and case studies to illustrate

3. Environmental Benefits
  ◦ Explanation of how plant-based diets reduce greenhouse gas emissions and other environmental impacts
  ◦ Examples and statistics to support (e.g. X% reduction in carbon footprint)
4. Ethical Benefits
  ◦ Discussion of animal welfare and suffering in factory farming
  ◦ Argument for plant-based diets as a more ethical and compassionate choice
5. Conclusion
  ◦ Recap of key benefits
  ◦ Call-to-action: Encourage readers to try incorporating more plant-based meals into their diets

With this outline in hand, you can start fleshing out each section with specific notes, examples, and arguments from your Zettelkasten, feeling confident and motivated by the wealth of relevant ideas and insights at your fingertips. By leveraging the power of your slip box in this way, you can overcome writer's block and generate fresh, compelling ideas for your writing projects on a regular basis.

7.2 Drafting and Revising with the Support of Your Note Network

Once you have a clear idea and outline for your writing project, the next step is to start drafting and revising your work. This is where the real magic of the Zettelkasten method comes into play, as you can draw upon the rich network of notes and ideas you've built up over time to support and enhance your writing process.

Here are some tips for using your Zettelkasten to draft and revise your writing:

1. **Write from your notes:** As you begin drafting each section of your outline, start by reviewing the relevant notes and ideas from your Zettelkasten. Copy and paste key quotes, examples, and arguments directly into your draft, using them as a foundation for your own writing and analysis. This can help you quickly generate a rough first draft that is grounded in your existing knowledge and research.

2. **Elaborate and expand:** Once you have a basic structure in place, start elaborating and expanding on each point, adding your own insights, interpretations, and examples to create a more comprehensive and persuasive argument. Use your notes as a starting point, but don't feel limited by them - feel free to explore new ideas and connections as they arise in the writing process.

3. **Revise and refine:** As you continue to draft and revise your work, keep referring back to your Zettelkasten for additional support and inspiration. If you find yourself stuck or unsure about a particular point, search your notes for relevant ideas or examples that could help clarify or strengthen your argument. If you notice gaps or weaknesses in your reasoning, look for notes that could help fill in those gaps or provide alternative perspectives.

4. **Link and connect:** As you integrate ideas and examples from your Zettelkasten into your writing, make sure to link back to the original notes in your draft. This could be as simple as including a reference or footnote with the note ID, or using a specific linking syntax (e.g. [[202305030012]]) to create a clickable link within your document. By maintaining these connections, you can easily trace the evolution of your ideas and arguments back to their original sources.

5. **Iterate and improve:** Writing is an iterative process, and your Zettelkasten can support you through multiple rounds of revision and refinement. As you receive feedback from others or identify areas for improvement in your own review, continue to consult your notes for additional ideas and insights that could help strengthen your work. Over time, you may find that your writing and your Zettelkasten evolve together, each informing and enhancing the other in a virtuous cycle of learning and creation.

Example: Let's return to the example of writing an article about the benefits of a plant-based diet. With your outline in hand, you might start drafting the introduction by reviewing your notes on personal anecdotes and health transformation stories:

When Emily switched to a plant-based diet three years ago, she never imagined the profound impact it would have on her health and well-being. "I had been struggling with chronic fatigue, digestive issues, and joint pain for years," she explains. "But within just a few weeks of cutting out animal products, I started to feel like a new person. My energy levels soared, my skin cleared up, and the pain in my joints practically disappeared." ([[202301300012]])

Emily's story is not unique. In fact, a growing body of research suggests that plant-based diets can offer significant health benefits, from reducing the risk of chronic diseases like heart disease and diabetes ([[202302100018]]) to promoting weight loss and improving overall well-being ([[202303250007]]). By focusing on whole, minimally processed plant foods like fruits, vegetables, legumes, and whole grains, individuals can tap into the power of nutrition to transform their health and their lives.

As you continue drafting and revising the article, you might find yourself referring back to your Zettelkasten for additional support and inspiration:

- In the section on environmental benefits, you might pull in statistics and examples from your notes on greenhouse gas emissions and the impact of animal agriculture ([[202301200041]], [[202302050016]]).

· In the section on ethical considerations, you might draw upon your notes on animal welfare and the conditions in factory farms to make a persuasive case for the moral imperative of plant-based eating ([[202303150008]]).

· As you revise and refine your work, you might notice areas where your arguments could be stronger or more nuanced. Searching your Zettelkasten for additional notes and ideas on these topics could help you fill in those gaps and create a more robust and well-supported piece.

Throughout the drafting and revision process, you might also find yourself capturing new notes and ideas inspired by your writing:

· A particularly powerful quote or statistic from one of your sources that you want to remember for future use ([[202305120034]])

· A new insight or connection that emerges as you're analyzing the relationship between diet and environmental sustainability ([[202305120035]])

· An idea for a follow-up article on the challenges and strategies for transitioning to a plant-based diet ([[202305120036]])

By capturing these new notes and linking them back to your original draft, you can create a rich, interconnected web of ideas that continues to grow and evolve over time. And as you publish your article and share it with others, you may find that it sparks new conversations and connections that feed back into your Zettelkasten, inspiring new avenues for research, writing, and creation.

7.3 Streamlining the Research and Citation Process with Your Zettelkasten

One of the most time-consuming and tedious aspects of any

writing project is the process of researching and citing sources. Whether you're working on an academic paper, a journalistic article, or a non-fiction book, you need to be able to find, evaluate, and integrate relevant information from a wide range of sources, while also properly attributing and documenting those sources in your final work.

This is another area where your Zettelkasten can be an invaluable tool, helping you streamline and simplify the research and citation process. By capturing and organizing your sources and notes in a centralized, easily searchable system, you can quickly find and access the information you need, when you need it, without getting bogged down in the details of citation styles and formatting.

Here are some tips for using your Zettelkasten to streamline your research and citation workflow:

1. **Capture bibliographic information:** Whenever you add a new source to your Zettelkasten, make sure to capture all the relevant bibliographic information (e.g. author, title, publication date, URL) in a consistent format. This could be as simple as including a references section at the bottom of each literature note, or using a specific template or plugin to automatically generate citations in your preferred style (e.g. APA, MLA, Chicago).

2. **Link sources to notes:** As you create permanent notes based on the ideas and information from your sources, make sure to link back to the original bibliography entry. This could be as simple as including a reference or footnote with the author and year (e.g. Smith, 2022), or using a specific linking syntax (e.g. [@Smith2022]) to create a clickable link to the full citation.

3. **Use keywords and tags:** In addition to linking sources to specific notes, consider using keywords and tags to categorize and organize your references by topic, type, or other relevant criteria. For example, you might tag

all sources related to a particular research question or argument, or categorize sources by their level of credibility or relevance to your project. This can make it easier to find and filter sources later on, as you're drafting and revising your work.

4. **Create literature notes and summaries:** As you read and process your sources, create literature notes that summarize the key ideas, findings, and arguments in your own words. These notes can serve as a quick reference and reminder of what you've learned from each source, without having to go back and re-read the original material. You can also use these summaries to help you identify patterns, connections, and gaps across different sources, which can inform your own analysis and arguments.

5. **Integrate and attribute:** When you're ready to incorporate ideas and information from your sources into your writing, refer back to your Zettelkasten to find the relevant notes and citations. Use the linked references and bibliographic information to properly attribute and cite each source in your text, following the appropriate style guide for your field or publication. By keeping your sources and citations organized and easily accessible in your Zettelkasten, you can save time and reduce the risk of errors or omissions in your final work.

Example: Let's say you're working on a research paper about the psychological effects of social media use, and you're using your Zettelkasten to capture and organize your sources and notes. As you come across a new article on the topic, you might create a literature note that includes the full bibliographic information in APA style:

Title: Social Media Use and Mental Health: A Review of the Literature Author(s): Smith, J., & Johnson, S. Year: 2022 Journal: Journal of Social Media Psychology Volume: 45 Issue: 3 Pages: 123-145 DOI: 10.1037/jsmp0000123

Main ideas: - Excessive social media use is associated with increased risk of depression, anxiety, and loneliness ([[202305150023]]). - Social comparison and FOMO (fear of missing out) are key mechanisms linking social media use to negative mental health outcomes ([[202305150024]]). - Interventions that promote mindful and intentional social media use can help mitigate these negative effects ([[202305150025]]).

You might then create a set of permanent notes that elaborate on these key ideas, linking back to the original literature note and citation:

Title: Social Media and Risk of Depression Several studies have found a significant association between excessive social media use and increased risk of depression and other mental health problems (Smith & Johnson, 2022, [[202305150023]]). One possible explanation for this link is the phenomenon of social comparison ([[202305150024]]), where individuals compare their own lives and achievements to the curated highlight reels presented by others on social media. This constant comparison can lead to feelings of inadequacy, envy, and low self-esteem, which in turn can contribute to depressive symptoms.

As you continue researching and writing your paper, you can easily search your Zettelkasten for notes and citations related to specific keywords or tags (e.g. #socialmedia, #mentalhealth, #socialcomparison), and use the linked references to properly attribute and integrate the ideas and information into your arguments.

By using your Zettelkasten as a centralized hub for your research and citation process, you can save time, reduce cognitive load, and ensure that your final work is well-supported, properly attributed, and free of errors or omissions. And as you publish and share your work with others, you can continue to capture new ideas, feedback, and connections in your Zettelkasten, creating a virtuous cycle of learning, creation, and impact.

CONCLUSION

Over the course of this book, we've explored the power and potential of smart note-taking through the lens of the Zettelkasten method. We've seen how this approach, pioneered by Niklas Luhmann and refined by generations of knowledge workers, can transform the way we learn, think, and create, enabling us to unlock our full potential for insight, innovation, and impact.

At its core, the Zettelkasten method is about creating a personalized, lifelong system for capturing, organizing, and connecting the ideas and knowledge that matter most to us. By breaking down our thoughts and experiences into small, atomic notes, and deliberately linking and relating them to one another, we can create a rich, dynamic web of knowledge that grows and evolves alongside us, informing and inspiring our work and our lives.

Through the principles of atomicity, connectivity, and serendipity, the Zettelkasten method helps us overcome the limitations of rigid, linear thinking, and embrace a more fluid, associative approach to knowledge creation. By actively seeking out connections and patterns across different domains and disciplines, we can generate novel insights, spark creative breakthroughs, and develop a more nuanced, holistic understanding of the world around us.

But the real power of the Zettelkasten method lies not just in its theoretical principles, but in its practical application. By implementing smart note-taking practices into our daily lives and work, we can reap the benefits of enhanced memory, increased productivity, and greater creative output. Whether we're writing a book, launching a business, or simply pursuing our passions and curiosities, the Zettelkasten method gives us the tools and frameworks we need to turn our ideas into reality.

Throughout this book, we've explored the various stages and components of the Zettelkasten method, from capturing fleeting notes and processing literature notes, to creating permanent notes and linking them together in meaningful ways. We've seen how outlining and mapping tools can help us structure and visualize our ideas, and how the method can support the entire writing and content creation process, from ideation and research to drafting and revision.

Perhaps most importantly, we've emphasized the importance of using the Zettelkasten method not just as a tool for personal productivity, but as a catalyst for lifelong learning, growth, and impact. By embracing the principles of deliberate practice, feedback, and iteration, we can continually refine and expand our knowledge bases, building up a valuable resource that we can draw upon for years to come.

As we've seen, the Zettelkasten method is particularly valuable in the context of entrepreneurship and business, where the ability to generate new ideas, spot emerging trends, and adapt to changing circumstances is essential for success. By capturing and connecting insights from a wide range of sources and perspectives, entrepreneurs can stay ahead of the curve, identify new opportunities for innovation and growth, and build more resilient, adaptive organizations.

And yet, the applications of smart note-taking extend far beyond the realm of business and professional success. By cultivating a habit of lifelong learning and knowledge creation, we can enrich our personal lives, deepen our understanding of the world, and contribute to the collective knowledge and wisdom of our communities and societies.

As we conclude this exploration of the Zettelkasten method, I encourage you to reflect on how you can integrate these principles and practices into your own life and work. Whether you're a student, a professional, an entrepreneur, or simply a curious and motivated learner, the power of smart note-taking is within your reach.

It may take time, effort, and patience to build up your Zettelkasten and develop your skills as a knowledge worker. But with persistence, practice, and a commitment to lifelong growth, you can unlock your full potential for insight, creativity, and impact, and make a meaningful difference in the world.

So start small, stay focused, and trust in the process. Embrace the joy and excitement of discovery, and let your curiosity guide you to new frontiers of knowledge and understanding. And above all, remember that the journey of a thousand notes begins with a single idea, captured and nurtured in your own personalized system for thinking and creating.

The future of learning, innovation, and success belongs to those who are willing to take smart notes. So take up your pen, open up your mind, and let the adventure begin.

Software and Tools:

1. Roam Research - A networked note-taking tool designed for capturing, connecting, and exploring ideas, with features like bidirectional linking and graph visualization.

2. Obsidian - A powerful, extensible note-taking app that supports Markdown formatting, linking, and customization, with a growing community of Zettelkasten users and developers.

3. The Archive - A simple, elegant note-taking app designed specifically for the Zettelkasten method, with features like plaintext formats, wiki-style linking, and keyboard navigation.

4. Zotero - A free, open-source reference management tool that can be used to capture, organize, and cite bibliographic information for your Zettelkasten sources.

Appendix B: Templates and Checklists for Implementing the

Zettelkasten Method

Fleeting Note Template:

- Date:
- Time:
- Location:
- Main Idea:
- Related Thoughts/Connections:
- Next Actions/Questions:

Literature Note Template:

- Source Title:
- Author(s):
- Publication Date:
- Main Arguments/Ideas:
    - Idea 1:
    - Idea 2:
    - Idea 3:
- Key Quotes/Examples:
    - Quote 1:
    - Quote 2:
- Related Notes/Connections:
- Followup Questions/Actions:

Permanent Note Template:

- Unique ID:
- Title:
- Main Idea:
- Supporting Arguments/Examples:
    - Argument 1:
    - Argument 2:
- Connections/Linked Notes:
    - Connection 1:

◦ Connection 2:

· Questions/Further Exploration:

Zettelkasten Setup Checklist:

1. Choose your note-taking tool(s)
2. Decide on a unique identifier system
3. Establish a consistent note format
4. Set up your folders/tags/categories
5. Create a reference/citation workflow
6. Develop a regular review/maintenance schedule
7. Start capturing fleeting and literature notes
8. Process notes into permanent notes within 24-48 hours
9. Link and connect notes as you process them
10. Use your Zettelkasten for writing, research, and knowledge creation

Appendix C: Frequently Asked Questions About Smart Note-Taking and Zettelkasten

1. **Q: Do I need to use a specific tool or software to implement the Zettelkasten method?**

A: No, you can use any tool that supports the basic principles of the Zettelkasten method, such as plaintext formats, unique identifiers, and linking between notes. Many people use analog tools like index cards and slip boxes, while others prefer digital apps like Roam Research, Obsidian, or The Archive. The key is to find a tool that works for your specific needs and workflows.

1. **Q: How many notes should I have in my Zettelkasten?**

A: There is no fixed number of notes that you "should" have in your Zettelkasten. The size of your collection will depend on your specific interests, projects, and goals. Some people have Zettelkastens with thousands of notes, while others may have just a few hundred. The key is to focus on quality over quantity, and to regularly review and maintain your notes to keep them relevant and valuable.

1. **Q: Can I use the Zettelkasten method for fiction writing or creative projects?**

A: Absolutely! While the Zettelkasten method is often associated with academic or non-fiction writing, many fiction writers and creatives also use the approach to capture and develop ideas, characters, plot points, and themes. The principles of atomicity, connectivity, and serendipity can be just as valuable for sparking new ideas and connections in creative work as they are in more analytical or research-based projects.

1. **Q: How do I prevent my Zettelkasten from becoming a disorganized mess over time?**

A: The key to maintaining an organized Zettelkasten is to establish clear principles and workflows from the outset, and to stick to them consistently over time. This includes things like using a consistent note format, regularly reviewing and processing your notes, and being intentional about the types of connections and links you create. It can also be helpful to use tags, categories, or other metadata to create higher-level structure and organization within your note collection.

1. **Q: Can I collaborate with others on a shared Zettelkasten?**

A: Yes, many people use shared or collaborative Zettelkastens to support teamwork, research, or writing projects. Tools like Roam Research and Obsidian support real-time collaboration and shared databases, while analog systems can be shared through physical card catalogs or file cabinets. The key is to establish clear guidelines and workflows for how notes will be captured, organized, and linked, and to ensure that all collaborators are trained and bought into the system.

1. **Q: How do I integrate my Zettelkasten with other productivity or knowledge management systems?**

A: The Zettelkasten method can be easily integrated with other productivity or knowledge management frameworks, such as GTD (Getting Things Done), PKM (Personal Knowledge

Management), or PARA (Projects, Areas, Resources, Archives). For example, you might use your Zettelkasten to capture and develop ideas for your GTD projects, or use your PKM system to manage the higher-level categories and areas of your Zettelkasten. The key is to find a balance and workflow that works for your specific needs and goals.

This content is provided for informational and educational purposes only and should not be construed as professional advice or a substitute for seeking appropriate professional assistance.

The information presented herein is based on the authors' personal experiences, research, and opinions, which may not be suitable or applicable for all individuals or situations.

The authors, publishers, and distributors have made reasonable efforts to ensure the accuracy and timeliness of the information contained herein. However, they do not guarantee the completeness, suitability, or applicability of this information for any specific individual, situation, or purpose. The authors, publishers, and distributors shall not be held liable for any direct, indirect, incidental, or consequential damages resulting from the use or misuse of the information provided.

It is strongly recommended that readers seek professional advice and guidance from qualified professionals in their respective fields, such as financial advisors, legal counsel, medical practitioners, or certified coaches, for their specific situations and needs.

No part of this content may be reproduced, distributed, or transmitted in any form or by any means, including photocopying, recording, or other electronic or mechanical methods, without the prior written permission of the authors or copyright holders.

For other books and resources that may interest you, please click here:

https://know.howtoalways.win/raissagomez

Made in the USA
Middletown, DE
11 September 2024

60663183R00040